WHAT HAPPENS WHEN I FLUSH THE TOILET?

By Walter LaPlante

Gareth Stevens
PUBLISHING

Please visit our website, www.garethstevens.com. For a free color catalog of all our high-quality books, call toll free 1-800-542-2595 or fax 1-877-542-2596.

Library of Congress Cataloging-in-Publication Data

LaPlante, Walter, author.
 What happens when I flush the toilet? / Walter LaPlante.
    pages cm — (Everyday mysteries)
 Includes index.
 ISBN 978-1-4824-3825-3 (pbk.)
 ISBN 978-1-4824-3826-0 (6 pack)
 ISBN 978-1-4824-3827-7 (library binding)
 1. Toilets—Juvenile literature. 2. Sewage disposal—Juvenile literature. I. Title. II.
Series: Everyday mysteries.
 TH6498.L37 2016
 644'.6—dc23
                                    2015025576

Published in 2016 by
Gareth Stevens Publishing
111 East 14th Street, Suite 349
New York, NY 10003

Copyright © 2016 Gareth Stevens Publishing

Designer: Katelyn E. Reynolds
Editor: Kristen Nelson

Photo credits: Cover, pp. 1, 5 saknakorn/Shutterstock.com; pp. 3–24 (background) Natutik/Shutterstock.com; p. 7 Designua/Shutterstock.com; p. 9 Andrey_Kuzmin/ Shutterstock.com; p. 11 AuntSpray/Shutterstock.com; p. 13 hans engbers/ Shutterstock.com; p. 15 Jaromir Chalabala/Shutterstock.com; p. 17 Federico Rostagno/Shutterstock.com; p. 19 Pachanon/Shutterstock.com.

Printed in the United States of America

CPSIA compliance information: Batch #CW16GS: For further information contact Gareth Stevens, New York, New York at 1-800-542-2595.

CONTENTS

Bathroom Mystery 4

Inside the Tank. 6

Septic Tanks and Sewers 10

Clean It Up! 14

Low Flow 18

Don't Flush It All! 20

Glossary. 22

For More Information 23

Index 24

Boldface words appear in the glossary.

Bathroom Mystery

Once you press down on the handle on a toilet, the waste in the bowl is washed away! Have you ever wondered how that happens? Or where wastewater goes after you **flush** the toilet?

4

Inside the Tank

A toilet's handle has an arm tied to a chain or rod inside the toilet **tank**. This is joined to a **plug** called a flapper. Pressing down on the handle causes the chain or rod to lift the flapper.

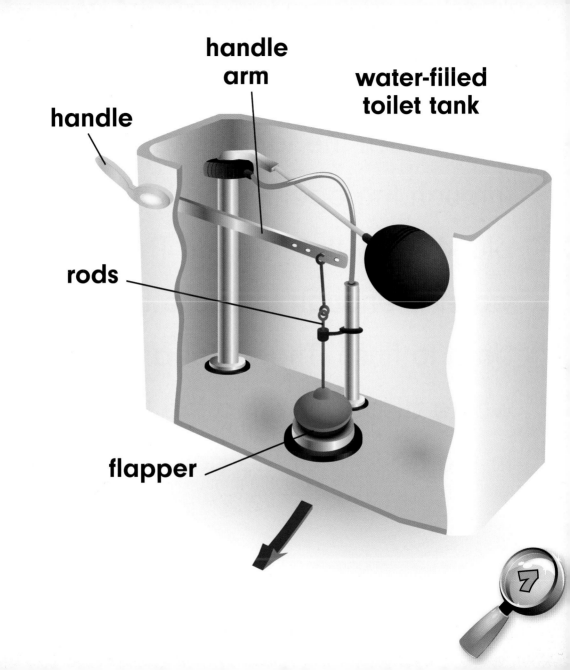

handle

handle arm

water-filled toilet tank

rods

flapper

Water from the tank flows through the opening no longer plugged by the flapper. The water is enough to cause the bowl to flush. The water and waste disappear into the hole in the bottom of the bowl!

Septic Tanks and Sewers

Toilet water leaves the house through pipes. The pipes may lead to a huge tank in the ground called a septic tank. Solid waste is sorted out, while the rest of the wastewater flows through a **drain** field that cleans it.

after flush

drain field

septic tank

11

In most cities and neighborhoods, toilet water flows into a bigger system of pipes called sewers. The main pipes are under the sidewalks and streets! Wastewater travels through the sewers until it reaches water **treatment** plants.

Clean It Up!

Water treatment plants clean wastewater! Some just sort out the solid waste. Others do this plus use bacteria to eat other unclean matter in the wastewater. Then the bacteria are removed. Some plants use **chemicals** to clean the water even more.

water treatment plant

15

Would you drink toilet water? You might and not know! Once cleaned, wastewater may become part of the water supply we drink from and bathe with. It might be used to water crops or go into rivers or lakes, too.

Low Flow

Older toilets use a lot of water to flush. Today, many toilets are called "low flow," meaning they use less water. They may even use buttons to flush! One makes more water flow into the bowl than the other.

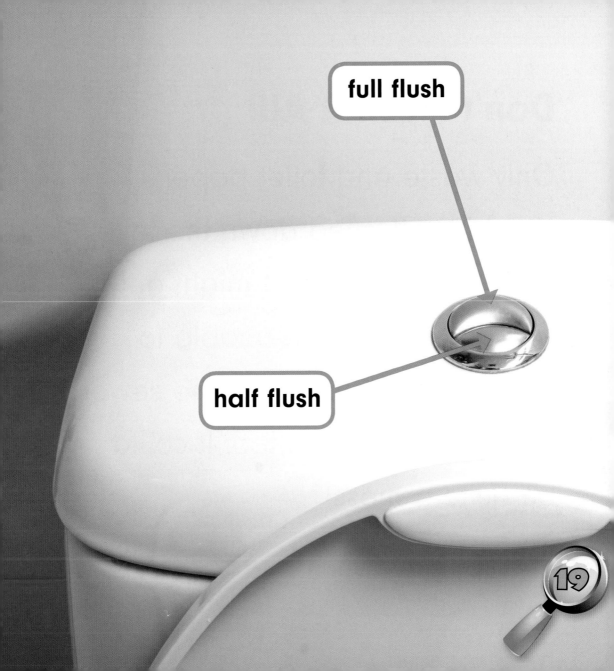

full flush

half flush

19

Don't Flush It All!

Only waste and toilet paper should be flushed down the toilet. Otherwise, your toilet might get plugged up and be unable to flush well. It could harm the sewer pipe or septic tank, too. It could be quite a mess!

FROM WASTEWATER TO DRINKING WATER

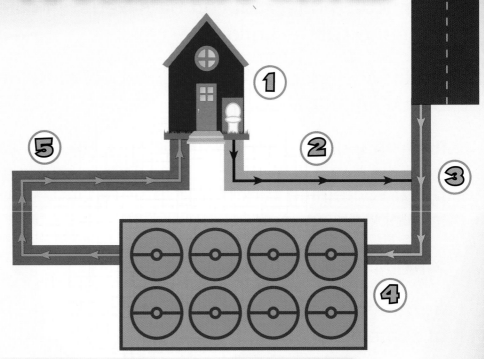

1. Wastewater is flushed down the toilet.

2. Wastewater leaves the house through a pipe.

3. Home pipes connect to the sewer system.

4. Wastewater is cleaned at a water treatment plant.

5. Water is returned to the water supply.

21

GLOSSARY

chemical: matter that can be mixed with other matter to cause changes

drain: having to do with the removal of a liquid by letting it flow away

flush: to cause a sudden flow of water

plug: something that blocks an opening. Also, to block an opening.

tank: something that holds a liquid

treatment: having to do with the handling of something

FOR MORE INFORMATION

BOOKS

Lynette, Rachel. *Toilet Paper Before the Store*. Mankato, MN: The Child's World, 2012.

Macdonald, Fiona. *You Wouldn't Want to Live Without Toilets!* New York, NY: Franklin Watts, 2015.

WEBSITES

How Do Toilets Work in Space?
iss.jaxa.jp/kids/en/life/04.html
Now you know how toilets flush on Earth. Learn how toilets flush—and more—on the International Space Station!

Where Does Water Go?
dcwater.com/kids/activities/wheredoeswatergo.html
How much water do people use every day? Find out that and more!

INDEX

bacteria 14

bowl 4, 8, 18

buttons 18

chain 6

chemicals 14

drain field 10

flapper 6, 8

handle 4, 6

low flow 18

pipes 10, 12, 20, 21

rod 6

septic tank 10, 20

sewers 12, 20, 21

tank 6, 8

toilet paper 20

waste 4, 8, 10, 14, 20

wastewater 4, 10, 12, 14, 16, 21

water supply 16, 21

water treatment plants 12, 14, 21